A SOUL ON FIRE FOR THE LORD

From the Living Water Ministries Church of God in Christ

REVEREND RENE JOHNSON

ISBN 979-8-88616-583-8 (paperback)
ISBN 979-8-88616-584-5 (digital)

Christian Faith Publishing, Inc.
832 Park Avenue
Meadville, PA 16335
www.christianfaithpublishing.com

Printed in the United States of America

FOREWORD

My name is Nelson Silver. I'm a Jewish American businessman in the transportation industry in Los Angeles! I first met Reverend Rene Johnson when I was seventeen years old and Rene was sixteen years old at Hamilton High School. He was a cool Black kid who played baseball in school. He loved baseball—I know that—and Nelson was a pretty good hockey player. So, we bonded on that alone, and he met my family, and I met his family. His family was Black, and mine was Jewish White. But as our friendship evolved, my family grew to love Rene too. We—my family and I—found out quickly that Rene had a gift in selling, and he began to work with us, the Silvers, in our family-owned business in Los Angeles (Avon Rent-a-Car-Truck-Van) while still chasing his dream of playing Major League Baseball. Rene eventually gave up baseball and became our top leading salesman after battles with drug addiction and prison time. I'm proud of who Rene has become and I his lifelong friend. He is now truly a man of God; he gives all glory to the Lord!

Rene graduated from multiple ministry and theology courses in and out of prison, and anyone can see he is anointed and called by God to be used by God to bless others with the power God has anointed him with and where God positioned him. He is now truly Reverend Rene Johnson, and I've witnessed his soul being on fire for the Lord.

Nelson Silver
Lifelong friend and mentor

FIRE STARTER

Jesus the Lord is the way. God bless you and your family abundantly, according to all his riches in glory by Christ Jesus in every area of your lives (Philippians 4:19). That is God's desire for each and every one of his children. God loves you like no one else can. If you have this book in your hand and you've never met Jesus Christ the Lord and Savior of your life, you need to do so! God loves you. And he cares for you so much that he sent his only Son, Jesus, to be sacrificed for you. He loves you so much that he also sent his powerful Holy Spirit into the earth to be your Comforter and Teacher. He loves you so much he has made it so that you can live free from sickness or disease. God desires only the best for you. Believe it. Make the choice today to begin to receive the best God has in store for your life in every area of it. God, for whom it is impossible to lie, says so in his Word (Hebrews 6:18). It is his gift to you! Ask and receive it! *Let your soul be on fire for the Lord!* Amen.

Prayer of Salvation

Join me in saying this prayer today. Don't just read it. Repeat these words out loud:

> *Heavenly Father, in the name of Jesus, I come*
> *before you. I confess to you I am a sinner. I ask you*
> *to forgive me. I believe Jesus, your only begotten*
> *Son, died for my sins and that he rose from the*

dead. From this moment I ask Jesus to come into my heart. I make him my Lord and Savior! Amen!

Beloved, if you said this prayer out loud, you are now born again and no longer separated from God, and you are a Christian. You are a child of the almighty God! Now begin to *praise God* every day for making you his child. Colossians 1:12–14 says, "Giving thanks to the Father who has qualified us to be partakers of the *inheritance* of the saints in *the light*. He has delivered us from the power of darkness and conveyed us into the kingdom of the Son of his love, in whom we have redemption through his blood, the forgiveness of sins" (emphasis mine). Beloved, you have just inherited the kingdom of God. 1 John 3:2 says, "Beloved, *now* we are children of God" (emphasis mine). You can receive all God has promised starting right now! You are in the kingdom, the family of God. Now that you are in his family, you need to know *all* about your Father in heaven, the One who has changed you and made you new, who rebirthed you in your spirit, through the power of his powerful Holy Spirit. You need to know what your full inheritance is and how to walk in it.

How to Walk Every Day with Your Soul on Fire for the Lord!

In the next chapter, I will show you how you can now receive his greatest blessings in every area of your life, by the same *power* and *anointing* that was on Jesus, that will empower you to be a success in your new life and walk as a child of God; to be full of his joy and love, understanding, and overcoming power; and to be victorious in all you put your hands to do! Amen. Please join me in setting your soul on fire for the Lord!

God Is the Holy Spirit

Beloved, you now have God's Holy Spirit indwelling in you! It is by the power of the Holy Spirit that you can profess with your mouth Jesus is your Lord and Savior. Romans 10:9 tells us that *if* you confess with *your mouth the Lord Jesus* and *believe* in your heart that God has raised him from the dead, you will be saved. 1 Corinthians 12:3 says that no one can say Jesus is Lord except by the Holy Spirit. Jesus came to make it possible for man to receive the nature of God, which is eternal life. John 3:16 says, "For God so loved the world [the man he created and put in the world] that he gave his only begotten Son that *whoever believes in him* should *not perish* but have *everlasting life*" (emphasis mine). And, beloved, he also came so we can have life and have it more abundantly now! John 10:10 says, "The thief [Satan] does not come except to steal and to kill and to destroy. I have come that they [us] may have life, and that they may have it *more abundantly*" (emphasis mine). Jesus said in Mark 10:29–30, "Assuredly I say to you, there is no one who has left house or brothers or sisters or father or mother or wife or children or lands, for my sake and the gospels, who shall not receive a hundredfold *now* in this time—houses and brothers and sisters and mothers and children and lands with persecutions—and in the age to come, eternal life" (emphasis mine). What Jesus was saying in this scripture is when you put him first before everything and everyone in your life to follow him and his purpose for your life and walk, to do your service for the kingdom of God, he will bless you in every area of your life a hundredfold more than the abundance you had before you made him your Lord and Savior, right now and in the age to come, eternal life. Mark alone mentions you will have persecutions in this life for sure (trials and tribulations), but Jesus said in regard to this in John 16:33, "These things I have spoken to you, that *in me you may have peace. In the world* you will have tribulation, but be of good cheer, *I have overcome the world*" (emphasis mine).

A man could not be born again while Jesus was on the earth. He had power here to forgive sins, but there could be no new creation until he paid the price on Calvary and became the firstborn from the dead (died and rose again).

In John 16:7, 12–15, Jesus said:

> Nevertheless I tell you that it's the truth, it is to your advantage that I go away, the helper will not come to you: but if I depart, I will send him to you.
>
> I have yet still many things to say to you but you cannot bear them now, However, when *He, the spirit of truth*, has come, *he* will *guide* you into *all truth*: for he will not speak *on his own authority*, but whatever he hears he will *speak*: *He* will tell you things to come, He will glorify Me, for He will take of what is mine and declare it to you. All things that the *Father* has are mine; Therefore I said that he will take of mine and declare it to you. (emphasis mine)

Jesus told this to the disciples who walked with him by his side for the three years of his earthly ministry. (There were 120 men besides the *chosen twelve he made apostles* as well.) He told them it was more profitable for them if he went away and sent to them the *Holy Spirit*. Beloved, it is the work of the Holy Spirit (the same one he sent after his death and resurrection at Calvary) that has now made you a *new creation in Christ* (see 2 Corinthians 5:17) when you made Jesus the Lord over your life. The Holy Spirit came into you at that moment and now indwells in you! See John 14:17.

Beloved, the *Word* of God is spirit and truth, and it is the light of life. Everything in our life is in the Word of God. By it everything consists of our relationship with the Father, the Son (Christ), and the Holy Spirit, the triune of God. They are three but one, and they bear witness of each other in heaven (1 John 5:7). When we follow and obey the Word of God, our joy is complete in him. We are blessed abundantly in every area of our lives. And we are able to walk with our soul on fire for the Lord!

RESTING OUR SOUL IN CHRIST JESUS

My brethren, though you may be new members to the kingdom of God, perhaps even in passing from time to time because of the travel of the prophetic Word of God, you probably heard or even know some of God's more popular and repeated scriptures from the Holy Bible, the most recognized book in the world. One of those scriptures from the book of John is found in chapter 14, verse 5, when Thomas, one of the twelve chosen disciples of Jesus, asked Jesus, "Lord, we don't know where you are going, and how can we know the way?" In verse 6, Jesus said to him, "I am the way, the truth, and the life. No one comes to the Father except through me." Jesus was saying to Thomas (and to all the body of Christ) that he is the way to holiness, righteousness, love, and abundance. When we walk the way he did, we walk into all truth in every area of our lives. And when we follow his path, it leads to life, an even more abundant one. We are in fellowship constantly with the Father, the Son, and the Holy Spirit. We release all of God's supernatural power into all our circumstances pertaining to life, because when you seek to follow the example Jesus set for us all, you walk in obedience to the Word of God. Therefore, you align your will with God's will. And he always leads us to triumph and victory in our lives. You are his child. What human father doesn't want the very best for his child? So even more so, your heavenly Father wants the very best for you in every area of your life.

2 Corinthians 2:14 says, "Now thanks be to God who always leads us in triumph in Christ Jesus, and through us diffuses the fragrance of his knowledge in every place." *God is spirit!* See John

4:24. Those who worship him must worship in spirit and truth. Beloved, the real you is spirit. You have a soul and a body. Our soul consists of our *will, emotions, imagination,* and *intellect* (mind). Beloved, when we are walking in Jesus, essentially we are walking in the Word of God, doing what it says, putting it into action every day in our lives. Jesus said in Matthew 6:33, "But seek first the kingdom of God and his righteousness, and all these things will be added to you." Jesus was speaking of his followers to seek to live a holy life, to seek to live the righteousness of the Father, to set the mind on the things of God and not the things of the earth. Colossians 3:1–3 says, "If then you were raised with Christ seek those things which are above, where Christ is sitting at the right hand of God. Set your mind on things above, not on things of the earth. For you died [to the former way you lived] and your life is hidden with Christ in God!" So now you can walk with your soul on fire for the Lord!

So, beloved, when our souls are filled with the things of Christ, our will and thoughts are centered on him and his ways. And thus we are able to control our emotions instead of them controlling us, and our thoughts are being directed by the Holy Spirit, and he guides us to the way we should go. We then release God's blessings into our lives because he sees he can trust us to be obedient to his statutes and commandments (his will for our lives to fulfill his purpose for our lives). Jeremiah 29:11 says, "For I know the thoughts that I think toward you, says the Lord, thoughts of peace and not of evil to give you a future and a hope." Verses 12–13 say, "Then you will call upon me and go and pray to me, and I will listen to you. And you will seek me and find me, when you search for me with all your heart." God looks at the heart, not at the outward appearance of man. He doesn't see like man sees. Man only looks at the outward appearance of things. See 1 Samuel 16:7: "But the Lord said to Samuel, 'Don't look at his appearance or at his physical stature, because I have refused him. For the Lord does not see as man sees, for man looks at the outward appearance, but the Lord looks at the heart.'"

Brethren, children of God, listen up! "All Scripture [Word of God] is given by inspiration of God [it's God-breathed] and is profitable for doctrine, for reproof, for correction, and for instruction in righteousness that the man of God may be complete thoroughly, equipped for every good work" (2 Timothy 3:16–17). My friends in the body of Christ, I want for you to understand the God we now serve after we made Jesus our Lord and Savior is a God of peace and order, not confusion. See 1 Corinthians 14:33.

As I shared with you earlier, God wants the very best for all his children in every area of their lives. God Almighty, the Creator of the heavens and earth, loves you! With an agape kind of love (this kind of love is unconditional and forever), he never changes; it is not in his nature. Malachi 3:6 says, For *I am the Lord, I do not change!*" (emphasis mine). He desires us to walk in his ways in holiness and righteousness. He wants to bless you abundantly with the desires of your heart. Amen. Psalm 37:4 says, "Delight yourself also in the Lord, And he shall give you the desires of you heart." It doesn't say he might give you the desires of your heart; it says he shall give them to you! So, my fellow brethren in the body of Christ, which you are members of, I beseech you to delight yourselves in God through prayer, through study of his Word every day, by praising him continually out of your mouths every day and doing what the apostle Paul said to do in 1 Corinthians 14:40, "Let all things be done decently and in order." We are God's workmanship, created in Christ Jesus for good works, which God prepared beforehand that *we should walk in them.* See Ephesians 2:10. Let's continue to surrender our will to the Lord's will, to trust him, and to acknowledge him in all our ways (Proverbs 3:6). Beloved, he will direct and already is directing our paths! Amen. Let's allow the workings of the Holy Spirit to set our souls on fire for the Lord!

Jesus, Our Source for Prosperity

Brethren, listen up!

> Thus *says* the Lord your Redeemer the holy one of Israel: *I am* the *Lord your God who teaches* you to *profit, who leads* you by the way *you should* go. (Isaiah 48:17, emphasis mine)

This scripture is talking about Jesus. He is the One who prospers our soul. He is the One who says, "I'll teach you how to profit!" He does this through the Word of God! Jesus is the Word (John 1:1). John 1:14 says, "And the *Word* became *flesh* and *dwelt* among us" (emphasis mine)—Jesus, who in John 14:6 told us he is the way, the truth, and the life! He leads us to holiness; to all truth, to have a godly life, a joyful life, a more abundant life (John 10:10); and to prosperity in every area of our lives, spiritual, physical, and financial. No one else can do it! In John 15:5 Jesus said, "For without me you can do nothing." Let us, who are now in Jesus and have made him our Lord and Savior, make it our fundamental aim to walk as he walked. 1 Peter 2:21 says, "For to this you were called because *Christ also* suffered for us *leaving* us an *example* that you should *follow his steps*" (emphasis mine). In 3 John 1:2, the apostle John said, "Beloved, I pray that *you* [us] may *prosper* in *all things* and be in health just as your *soul prospers*" (emphasis mine). 3 John 1:11 says, "Beloved, do not imitate [follow] what is evil, but what is good. *He who does good* [follows] is of *God*, but he who does evil has not seen God" (emphasis mine). (John was speaking of *spiritually seeing*.)

Beloved, prosperity is intended by God for every area of our lives. Amen! 2 Corinthians 8:9 says, "For you know the grace of our Lord Jesus Christ, that though he was rich, yet for our sakes he became poor that through his poverty that we may become rich."

Beloved, when the apostle John said we should prosper in health, even as thy soul prospered, in 3 John 1:2, he knew man is *spirit*. He has a *soul* consisting of the mind, will, emotions, imagination, and intellect. And he lives in a fleshly *body* (1 Thessalonians 5:23). So there is *spiritual prosperity* first, then *mental* (soul) *prosperity*, and *physical prosperity*. To prosper spiritually, we must be born again. When we accept Jesus as our Lord and Savior and ask him into our heart, our spirit is reborn. Amen! Then we bring our self into fellowship and alignment with our heavenly Father. This now puts us in a position to receive from God all that he promised in his Word. To prosper in our soul, we must be able to control our mind, our will, and our emotions. Brethren, just because we've learned a great amount of knowledge doesn't mean that now our mind is prosperous; it means we gained knowledge to our mind. Prosperity of our mind comes when we use the knowledge we've ascertained—when we are controlling our mind rather than our mind controlling us. 2 Corinthians 10:5 tells us we are to cast down arguments (imaginations = thoughts) and every high thing that exalts itself against the knowledge of God, bringing every thought into captivity to the obedience of Christ. Beloved, when we do this, we position ourselves to prosper mentally.

Beloved, we cannot control our minds completely without the Word of God being alive and operating inside of us. The Word of God (which is God [John 1:1]) and his Holy Spirit teach us and guide us in the way to control our will and emotions (our thought life). Remember the enemy can only attack you in your mind with thoughts, ideas, and suggestions. This is why God's Word instructs us in 2 Corinthians 10:5 to bring every thought that goes against the Holy Spirit into captivity to the obedience of Christ (his Word). Amen! By doing this we allow the Holy Spirit's guidance into the prosperity that God wants for each and every one of his beloved children (us)! Beloved, God wants us all to have true prosperity in every area of our lives. This is why we must be diligent to walk in the Lord's ways and make it our aim every day to seek him early. Psalm 34:10 says, "But those who *seek the Lord shall not lack any good thing*" (emphasis mine). Jesus said he will give us the keys to the kingdom of heaven (Matthew 16:19). He also said, "But seek the kingdom of God [through his Word] and all these things will be added to you. For it is your Father's [God] good pleasure to give you the kingdom" (Luke 12:31–32).

Some of us forget it is God who supplies all our needs according to his riches in glory by Christ Jesus (Philippians 4:19). Deuteronomy 8:17–18 says, "Then you say in your heart, my power and might of my hand have gained me wealth. But you shall remember the Lord your God, it is *he* who gives us the *power* to get *wealth*!" (emphasis mine). Money is a good thing when used in a godly fashion and manner, to uplift and provide for one's family, to give help to those in need in the body of Christ, and to tithe in our churches (joined together with our church). God knows it costs money to *spread* his Word (gospel) and will prosper those so joined in doing so. He knows who is a faithful servant and who is not! He knows and sees our hearts fully. Hebrews 4:13 tells us no creature is hidden "from his sight but *all things* are naked and *open* to the eyes of him to whom *we must* give *account*" (emphasis mine). Verse 12 says the Word (God) of God is living and powerful (all-powerful) and sharper than any two-edged sword and is a discerner (all-knowing) of the thoughts and intents of the heart. So, brethren, he knows whom he can trust with his riches! Amen. Money is not the root of all evil. The love of money is the root of all evil (1 Timothy 6:10). James, who was Jesus's half brother, testified in James 4:3, "*You ask* and *do not receive* because you ask amiss [*amiss* means 'in an improper way'] that you may *spend* it *on your pleasures*!" (emphasis mine). Therefore, beloved, submit to God's ways (follow him). And the spirit of the disobedient one (the devil, evil) will free from you! Amen! From now on, brethren, let us make it our aim to follow Jesus. He will lead us into prosperity in all areas of our lives. Amen! This message is brought to you by the Living Water Ministries Church of God in Christ!

WE WALK IN JESUS

Brethren, you are the body of Christ. One of my favorite scriptures is John 15:5, where Jesus said, "I am the vine, you are the branches [you and me]. He who abides in me, and I in him, bears much fruit; for *without me you can do nothing!*" (emphasis mine). This scripture tells us now that we have made Jesus our Lord and Savior, we have certain rights! He is now abiding in us, and we are in him. In John 15:7–8 Jesus said, "If you abide in me and my words abide in you, you will ask what you desire and it shall be done for you. By this My Father is glorified, that you bear much fruit, so you will be my disciples." Beloved, the Son of the living God is abiding in you, and we are abiding in him. When we walk now, we walk in him spiritually, and his powerful Holy Spirit is guiding us into abundance supernaturally that we will bear much fruit. This glorifies the Father! He is full of joy to see us walk in him, and he is joyful to abide in us! John 15:11 says, "These things I have spoken to you, that *my joy may remain in you*, and that *your joy may be full*" (emphasis mine). Jesus the Christ wants you and me, beloved, his children, to walk every day with our souls on fire for the Lord.

Now that you are a born-again Christian (*Christian* is defined as "one who is Christlike"), you, as I indicated to you earlier in this book, have rights just like you have certain rights in the natural world, humanitarian rights and governmental rights. Wherever you reside, whatever country or city you may be in, there are certain rights afforded to its citizens. In Jesus Christ, you now have spiritual supernatural rights. John 1:12–13 says, "But as many as received him [Jesus], *to them he gave the right* to become *children of God*, to those who *believed* in his *name: who were born*, not of blood nor of the will of the flesh, nor of the will of man, *but of God!*" (emphasis mine). My friends, now that we are in Jesus, everywhere we move and in everything we do, we have the right to do it in the name of Jesus! Acts 17:26–28 says:

> And *He has made from one blood every nation of men* to dwell on all the face of the earth, and has determined their preappointed times and the boundaries of their dwellings, so they should seek the Lord in the hope that they might grope for him and find him, *though he is not far from each one of us; for in him we live* and *move* and *have our being* as also some of your own poets have said, "For we are also his offspring." (emphasis mine)

Scripture says you and I live and move and have our being in him! There is nothing, brothers and sisters, we can't do! We walk and move in the living all-powerful God of the universe, and he is with us and for us, and we have his omnipotence available readily in all we endeavor to do. Romans 8:31–32 says, "What then shall we say to these things? If God is for us, who can be against us? He [God] who did not spare his own son but delivered him up for us all, how shall he not with him also freely give us *all* things?" (emphasis mine). This is the gospel (good news!), my brethren in Christ. And he chose us to be in him before the foundation of the world that we should be holy and without blame before him in love, having predestined us to be adopted as sons by Jesus Christ to himself according to the good pleasure of his will. So, beloved, our Father in heaven loves and cares for you so much! He pleasures in the prosperity of his servants, us, who are born again in Christ Jesus. Amen!

See Psalm 35:27. I tell you truly, my beloved sisters and brothers in Christ, we must trust in the Lord Jesus Christ, with all our heart, all our soul and mind, and all our strength at all times in every area of our life, for he cares for us more than our earthly families ever can. He created us, beloved. He formed us in our mothers' wombs. He knows all our inner parts for he formed them when he covered us in our mothers' wombs. We must be praiseful to him continuously out of our mouths, being thankful for we are fearfully and wonderfully made. Marvelous are his works! That my soul knows very well. See Psalm 13 9:13–14. That being said I implore you to walk in Jesus every day for the rest of your earthly lives. Colossians 2:6–10 says:

> As you therefore have received Christ Jesus the Lord, so walk in him rooted and built in him and established in the faith as you have been taught, abounding in it with thanksgiving. Beware lest anyone cheat you through philosophy and empty deceit, according to the traditions of men, according to the basic principles of the world, and not according to Christ. For in him dwells all the fullness of the God head bodily. And you are complete in him, who is the head of all principality and power.

These verses tell us we don't need anyone in our lives that isn't in Christ also. He is our refuge. He is all we will ever need in this life and the one to come. Amen. Matthew 6:24 tells us in Jesus's words, "*No one* can serve two masters; for either he will hate the one and love the other, or else he will be loyal to the one and despise the other. *You cannot serve God and mammon*" (emphasis mine). I say to you right now as the beloved children of the almighty living God, all we will ever need we have right now, and it is Jesus Christ our Savior! So let us only walk by faith in him and never by sight (2 Corinthians 5:7). When we are doing this, our soul is on fire for the Lord!

Children of God, I say to you just as it is with the mind and body, so it is with the soul. There are certain things essentially needed for our soul's health and well-being. Each of us must attend to these things for one's self. We each must repent for our self. Each individual must apply Christ for one's self, and each of us must pray and speak to God. You must do this for yourself, for you to have your own personal relationship with Jesus Christ. Yes, I as a minister can pray for you, and it can be profitable for you, but you must do this first and foremost for yourself. Jesus said in Luke 18:1 that men *always ought to pray and not lose heart.*

In 1 Thessalonians 5:17, the apostle Paul instructed us to *pray without ceasing.* But it is important that when we pray, it is always in the spirit of belief, never ever doubting in our heart. This is the key! Jesus instructed us again in Mark 11:23–24 to have faith in God and believe: "For assuredly *I say to you,* whoever says to this mountain, be removed and be cast into the sea, and does not *doubt in his heart,* but *believes* that those things he says will be done he will have whatever he *says.* Therefore I say to you whatever things you ask *when you pray, believe* that you *receive them,* and *you will have them*" (emphasis mine). Notice it doesn't say you might have them. The word of God says you will have them! Our belief is the power and the key.

James, the brother of our Lord Jesus (see Matthew 13:55), instructed us:

> If any of you lacks wisdom, let him ask of God, who gives liberally and without reproach, and it will begiven to him. But let him ask in *faith* with *no doubting,* for he who *doubts* is like a wave of the sea driven and tossed by the wind. For let not that man suppose that he will receive anything from the Lord; he is a double-minded man, unstable in all his ways. (James 1:5:8, emphasis mine)

James was saying to us to not let our mind be divided by any doubt. *Double-minded* literally means "two souls." If one part of a person is set on God and the other is set on this world, there will be a constant conflict within. The true believer will trust in the Lord fully, with all belief! Our friend in the Lord, the apostle Paul, told us so in his letter to the Thessalonian church. For this reason, God will send them (anyone *who does not believe* and trust in Jesus Christ) strong delusion that they should believe the lie that they may all be condemned, those who did not believe the truth (God's Word) but had pleasure in unrighteousness. But we are bound to give thanks to God always, brethren, by the Lord because God from the beginning chose us for salvation through sanctification by the spirit and belief in the truth to which he called us by our gospel for the obtaining of the glory of our Lord Jesus Christ. Amen! Jesus wants us to walk only in belief in him, not the things of this world.

Beloved of God, we walk in belief in Jesus only with all our heart, all our soul, and all our strength. Deuteronomy 6:5–7 says, "You shall love the Lord your God with *all your heart, with all your soul* and *with all your strength*. And these words which I command you to day shall be *in your heart*. You shall teach them diligently to your children and shall talk of them when *you* sit in your house, when you walk by the way [wherever you may be at], when you lie down and when you rise up" (emphasis mine). God is telling us to walk in belief in him at all times with all our heart, soul, and strength. When we do this, beloved children of God, it releases all God's mighty blessings of abundance into our lives. Understand this is what causes to set our soul on fire for the Lord!

Beloved, God's Word is the truth and spirit. It is life. And it directs our paths when we are reading it, studying it, and speaking it. Then the Holy Spirit causes us to walk in it. In John 6:63–64 Jesus said, "It is the spirit who gives life; the flesh profits nothing. The words that I speak to you are *spirit*, and they are *life*. But there are some of you *who do not believe*" (emphasis mine). In John 6:65 Jesus said, "Therefore I have said to you that no one can come to me unless it has been granted to him by my Father." He also said this in a previous scripture: "No one can come to me unless the Father who sent me draws him and I will raise him up in the last day" (John 6:44).

We as the children of God are only satisfied in our soul when we are walking fully in all belief in the Word of God. It is righteousness, and it is true. Romans 10:17 says, "So then *faith comes by hearing*, and *hearing by the word of God*" (emphasis mine). This scripture tells us that the more we hear God's Word spoken into our ears, it increases our faith and causes true belief because the Holy Spirit bears witness with our soul that what we are hearing is truth. Romans 10:9–11 says, "That if you confess with your mouth the Lord Jesus and believe in your heart that God has raised Him from the dead, you will be saved. For with the heart one believes unto righteousness and with the mouth confession is made unto salvation. For scripture says, who ever believes on Him will not be put to shame." Jesus Christ is the only begotten Son of God, and whoever believes in him should never perish but have everlasting life, for God did not send his Son into the world to condemn the world but that the world through him might be saved. So, beloved, let us be obedient to the Word of God, standing in all belief of it!

> That you may walk worthy of the Lord, fully pleasing Him, being fruitful in every good work and increasing in the knowledge of God: strengthened with all might, according to His glorious power, for all patience and long suffering with joy; giving thanks to the Father who has qualified us to be partakers of the inheritance of the saints in the light. He has delivered us from the power of darkness and conveyed us into the Kingdom of the Son of His love, in whom we have redemption through His blood the forgiveness of sins. (Colossians 1:10–14)

These scriptures tell us God loves us so much he didn't even spare his only begotten Son but delivered him up for us, to save us from his wrath. He shed his precious blood for us because of his great love for us, beloved! He believes in us. Let's walk worthy of our Lord in believing in him with all our heart, all our soul, all our strength, and all our mind. Be a soul on fire for the Lord!

We Are Positioned for Authority

My dearly beloved brethren in Christ, I, Pastor Rene Johnson, the author of the book you are holding in your hand, wasn't always the authorities' man I am today, though I was baptized as a child early in my youth at the age of five or six and raised and reared in a Baptist church by my great-grandmother. Growing up the walking Bible I saw every day right before my eyes—an upright, holy, and just woman of God in every way. Even to this day, she is the most holy person I ever have seen. Tessie Mae Spencer (Nanny, as everyone affectionately called her—you would have, too, had you known her) walked in Christ every day of her life. She understood she was authorized by God to operate in the world of God with all authority! Of course she knew the Word of God, forward and backward, having studied and spoken it out into the atmosphere for over ninety odd years. But more importantly, she walked it out every day! I saw her feed the flock of God daily, not just family but strangers. She ministered to them with God's Word, healed and nursed everyone around her, and helped any and every one God brought in her path with their finances out of the blessings God gave her. She was never lacking anything ever. The Word says in Proverbs 28:27, "He who gives to the poor will not lack, but he who hides his eyes will have many curses." In Psalm 5:1–3 David (the prophet) said, "Give ear to my words, O Lord. Consider my meditation. Give heed to the voice of my cry, My king and My God, for to you I will pray. My voice you shall hear in the morning, o Lord; in the morning I will direct it to you, and I will look up." Beloved, my great-grandmother taught me to pray as a child. (The way to communicate with the Lord is through prayer and spirit.) So then as I said, the Word of God is truth and it is life! I bear witness of this, or my book would never have been published for it was by the power of God working through me that I was able to author this book. His Word gave me power and authority. This book is evidence of me *operating in the authority of God's Word.*

Proverbs 22:6 reads like this: "Train up a child in the way he should go, And when he is old he will not depart from it." My fellow brethren in Christ, the same authority and power Jesus used when he was here during his earthly ministry is available to you now that you have received Jesus as your Lord and Savior. When you did, you were given this authority (permission) to walk in all authority and power to operate in it just like he did! Scripture declares it to you. Read and understand and receive his Word and start walking in it! Luke 10:19 says, "Behold I *give you* the *authority* to trample on serpents and scorpions, and over all the power of the enemy [Satan] and nothing shall by any means hurt you" (emphasis mine). Though this is a great gift from the Father, it is to be used for good works and not any evil. Jesus went on to say in Luke 10:20, "Nevertheless do not rejoice in this, that the spirits are subject to you, but rather rejoice because your names are written in heaven."

The Word of God tells us in Jesus's own words he abides in us. And if you abide in him and his Word abides in you, you can ask what you desire, and it shall be done for you. *Abide* is defined as "to remain in place; to continue to be sure or firm, endure; to conform; to comply with; to remain." Jesus is in us, the only begotten of the Creator of the heavens and the earth and everything that's in existence, and he gives us the authority in him to operate just like he did on earth in all circumstances and also whenever you are attacked by the enemy (Satan). In Matthew 28:18 Jesus said, "All authority has been given to me in heaven and on earth." He gives us this authority; it is ours to use now! Let's go forth every day with strong courage knowing we walk in power and authority everywhere we tread our feet with our steps directed and ordered by the Lord Jesus Christ, for we are his offspring that we should walk in him every day with our soul on fire for the Lord!

PRAYER POWER

Jesus himself, during his earthly ministry here, was consistently in prayer. And the four gospels give account of this:

In Luke 18:1, Jesus said that men always ought to pray and not lose heart. He was saying pray and trust and believe with all thy heart God hears it and behave in a manner that you have received your request—as if it was done even before you've received it, because it is, as soon as God who sees our hearts knows you've believed it in your heart fully without doubting! Mark 11:22 says have faith in God!

Mark 11:24 says, "Therefore I say to you [us; this is Jesus speaking], *whatever things* you ask *in my name*, when you pray, *believe* that *you receive them_*and *you will have them!*" (emphasis mine). Jesus didn't say we might have them. He said we will have them! (Our belief is the key!) Jesus said he gave us the keys of the kingdom of heaven and whatever we bind on earth will be bound in heaven and whatever we loose on earth will be loosed in heaven. If you are a child of God, you have rights, and you have power!

> *But as many as received Him* [Jesus], *to them* He gave the *right* to become *children of God*, to those who *believe* in *His name!* (John 1:12, emphasis mine)

There's that big word again—*believe!* Without belief, there is no power! It is our belief that is the key to the kingdom and all its power! Without it you won't receive all of God! He will still bless you, yes, because he is sovereign and he is love! But he will not give you his all, and why should he when you aren't giving him your all when you have unbelief in your heart! There are mechanics to God's Word, and his way is not hard. It's only hard because we harden our hearts. Jesus said in Matthew 11:28–30, "*Come to me all you who labor and are heavy laden, and I will give you rest. Take my yoke upon you and learn from me, for I am gentle and lowly in heart and you will find rest for your souls. For My yoke is easy and my burden is light*" (emphasis mine). He didn't say his way is hard and his burden is heavy. He was saying he loves you and he's with you every step of your way so you don't stumble!

We, beloved, must study the Word of God to gain understanding in it. We must be diligent, obedient, faithful, and patient and ask God in prayer, by the power of the Holy Spirit, to give us wisdom and understanding of his Word. James, who was the brother of our Lord and Savior, Jesus Christ, the son of Mary and Joseph (Matthew 13:55), said in the book of James chapter 1, verses 5–8:

> If any of you lack wisdom let him ask God who gives to all liberally and without reproach [*reproach* means "no partiality"] and it will be given to him, but let him ask in faith [all belief] without doubting, for he who doubts is like a wave of the sea driven and tossed by the wind. For let not that man suppose that he will receive anything from the Lord; he is a double-minded man, unstable in all his ways.

Double-minded means to literally be led by two souls. He is divided and not a whole soul, one part set on God and one part set on the world. So therefore his soul is in conflict, not able to join fully with God. See Hebrews 3:18–19 where God said, "And to whom did he swear that they *would not enter His rest* but to those who did not obey? So we see that they could not enter in because of *unbelief*" (emphasis mine).

For indeed the gospel was preached to us as well as them, *but the word* [God is the Word (John 1:1)] which they heard *did not* profit them, not being mixed with faith [belief] in those who heard it. For we who have believed [the true children of God!] do enter that rest, as he has said [word], "So I swore in my wrath, they shall not enter My rest," although the works were finished from the foundation of the world! (Hebrews 4:2–3, emphasis mine)

Beloved, the Word tells us God chose us before he even formed the world to be in him!

Just as he chose us in him before the foundation of the world, that we should be holy and without blame before him in love, having predestined us [*predestined* means "ahead of time"] to adoption as sons and daughters by Jesus Christ to himself, according to the good pleasure of his will. (Ephesians 1:4–5)

We must understand who we are in Christ Jesus, beloved! Let's stop being carried away by the wisdom of men (the world) because man's wisdom is foolishness to God (1 Corinthians 3:19). Let our soul be on fire for the Lord!

Beloved, we can only truly communicate with God through our prayer! (*Communicate* comes from the word *commune*, which means literally "to come together"!) In Psalm 5:2–3 King David said, "Give heed to the voice of my cry, my King and my God, for to you *I will pray*. My voice you shall hear in the morning, O Lord! In the morning I will direct it to you, and I will look up!" (emphasis mine). In Psalm 55:16–17, David said again, "As for me, I will call upon God, and the Lord shall save me. *Evening* and *morning* and at *noon*, I will *pray* and cry aloud, and He shall hear my voice" (emphasis mine). David was confident in all belief his God (our

God too) heard his prayer, for he knew prayer only was heard from a believing heart! Jesus while on earth during his earthly ministry prayed constantly. See Matthew 14:23: "And when He had sent the multitudes away, he went up on the mountain by himself to pray. Now when evening came, he was alone there." (He spent the whole day praying!) Luke 6:12 tells us the account of him praying. It says, "Now it came to pass in those days that He went out to the mountain to *pray*, and *continued all night* in *prayer* to *God*!" (emphasis mine).

Beloved, I'm not saying you must pray around the clock. I'm saying it must be a fundamental part of your daily walk with the Lord. Prayer changes things. It allows God to communicate directly to you, to guide you by the workings of his Holy Spirit, to show you the way to go and the way not to go. It teaches you patience and persistence in the plans God has for your life. Prayer is powerful; it gives all power to every area of your life, so that you are a successful child of God! Remember God takes pleasure in seeing us his beloved prosper in *all* we do! Let us continue in prayer always without ceasing (1 Thessalonians 5:17). Let the mind that was in Christ Jesus (Philippians 2:5) also be in us! Let's keep our soul on fire for the Lord!

THE LOVE OF GOD

Any person who is in Christ is a new creation. He has been completely recreated. Old things are passed away; behold, all things have become new, and now all things are of God—not part of God and part of Satan. Some people think (and this is solely man's wisdom, which is foolishness to God) that when a man becomes a Christian, he has both the nature of God and the nature of Satan, but I assure you this is not so.

In the new birth, a man's spirit is completely reborn. It is then that man's responsibility to renew his mind. He can only do this by the Word of God and using the Word to take control of his spirit, soul, and body. See 1 Thessalonians 5:23. When you are reborn, now all things are of God, who has reconciled us to himself through Jesus Christ and has given the ministry of reconciliation. That is, God was in Christ reconciling the world to himself, not imputing their trespasses to them, and has committed to us the word of reconciliation. In Romans 12:2 the apostle Paul said, "And do not be conformed to this world [you're a new creation now!] but be transformed by the renewing of your mind that you may prove what is that good and acceptable and perfect will of God."

Beloved, as a pastor called and sent by a loving God and also a student of the Word of God, the word I got the most revelation from in Romans 12:2 was right at the end of the verse. And it was a single word—*that*. Let's look at it again: "*that* you may prove what is *that* good and acceptable and perfect will of God." Not our good or the world's definition of *good*, but the Word of God distinctively says, "what is *that* good." I interpret it as that good that is holy and completely acceptable in God's definition of *good*! Not what the world thinks is good or what we perceive to be good but only what is holy and acceptable to a loving and holy God, the God of our love. This is the good that can only come from love and through love, for God is love (1 John 4:8), and he who does not love does not know God. Nor can he ever know him, because everything in God's nature is love. What God has done throughout creation even up until now is out of love!

> *In this the love* of God was manifested toward us that God has sent his only begotten Son into the world, that we might *live through* him. *In this is love*, not that we loved God, but that he loved us and sent his Son to be the propitiation for our sins. Beloved, if God so loved us, we also ought to love one another. No one has seen God at any time, if we love one another, God abides in us and his love has been perfected in us. By *this* we know that we abide in him, and he in us because he has given us of his spirit [which is love!]. (1 John 4:9–13, emphasis mine)

> We have known and believed the love God has for us. God is love, and he who abides in love abides in God and God in him. Love has been *perfected*, among us *in this*, that we may have boldness in the day of judgement, because as he is, so are we in this world. (1 John 4:16–17, emphasis mine)

> We love him [God] because as he first loved us! (1 John 4:19)

Now, beloved, the Word of God is truly living and [quick] powerful, sharper than any two-edged sword. (In fact it is the sword of the spirit [Ephesians 6:17].) The first commandment in the Ten Commandments is to love (Deuteronomy 6:5). It says you shall love the Lord your God with all your heart, with all your soul, and with all your strength. Beloved, I have never counted yet how many times I've read the word *all* in the Word of God (the Holy Bible), but I assure you it must be thousands upon thousands. You see, God only does things one way. And it is all, or he doesn't do it! We don't serve a God who's with us part of the way or part of the time or in any way partly. He is with us all the time and all the way from the beginning to the end of our time here now and in the age to come, eternal life. He says so in his Word. And his Word is truth, spirit, and life!

We serve a God who is in love with us! The R&B group the O'Jays recorded a song called "A Mighty Love." Well, my friends, if you know God, what you have is a mighty love! Think about this. The Word of God says that he loved us even before the foundation of the world! In the natural, in man's finite way of thinking, it's really incomprehensible, but we can imagine it. Why? Because we were given the imagination characteristics of God by him. Remember Genesis 1:26: "Then God said, 'Let us make man in our image according to our likeness.'" The word *image* comes from the Greek and Latin word *imago*, which means "imagination." So we were made by the *imagination* of God, and he gave us part of that imagination when he made us spirit first! God is spirit (John 4:24). The Word says he knew us before he even formed us in our mothers' wombs! Jeremiah 1:5 says, "Before you were born I sanctified you." He loved you and sanctified you even before you were born! So let us walk in that love with the joy of God with us. Walk in the spirit of his love, which is in us. That's having a soul on fire for the Lord!

The Type of Man/ Woman God Uses

1. One who prays without ceasing (1 Thessalonians 5:17)
2. One who is faithful (Hebrews 11:6)
3. A giver of glory to God (1 Corinthians 10:31)
4. One who loves God's Word (Psalm 63)
5. One who doesn't give up when facing persecution (1 Corinthians 15:58)
6. One who is spirit-filled (Acts 7:55)
7. One who is born again (John 3:3)
8. One who is strong and courageous (Joshua 1:9)
9. One who is submitted to God (James 4:6)
10. One who is spirit-led (Romans 8:14)
11. One who is obedient to God's Word (1 Samuel 15:22–23)
12. One who is a good steward (Titus 1:7–8)
13. One who is a faithful servant (Matthew 25:14–28)
14. One who is available to God (Isaiah 6:8)
15. One who loves to praise his name (Psalm 57:1)

About the Author

Rene Johnson Sr. is the founding pastor of the Living Water Ministries Church of God in Christ in Los Angeles, California. He came fully into his calling in the ministry in 2013. He attended the Urban Ministry Institute (TUMI) and graduated top of his class and attended various other biblical courses and completed them, including nine Bible courses offered by the Salvation Army ministries also  in Los Angeles. He is actively and aggressively pursuing his building of the ministry in the love of God, guided by God's Holy Spirit, to do his part in the edifying of the body of Christ!